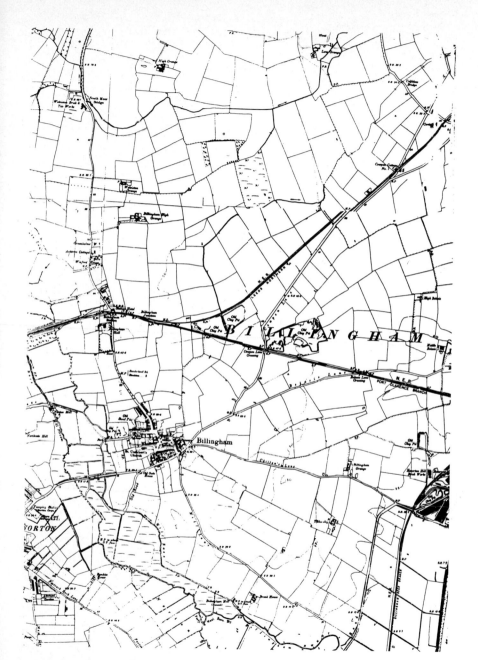

Although this is an extract from the Ordnance Survey Map of 1923 it illustrates Billingham in the days immediately prior to the First World War rather than in the 1920's because the map was based on a 1913 survey. However it does show that even before the coming of industry in the 1920's, that the village was expanding beyond its traditional limits. New buildings in Station Road north of the Green, and developments close to Billingham station, all illustrate that the village was no longer merely a nucleus of buildings standing around the Green. (Reproduced from the 6 inch Ordnance Survey Map, Sheets 44SE, 44SW, 50NE and 51NW, Durham, with the permission of the Controller of H.M.S.O., Crown Copyright Reserved).

BILLINGHAM IN TIMES PAST VOL. 2
INTRODUCTION

When I first began Volume One of this photographic history of the growth of Billingham from village to modern town, it was thought that this second volume would be the final volume and as such, cover the period from about 1920 to the present time. However, such was the success of Volume One that it was obviously clear that here was a story of urban development of great interest. Thus, this second volume covers only the period up to 1939, the period of the first stages of development, the coming of industry, the initial expansion of the village settlement and the creation of the first 'town'.

A further reason for the shorter period of time covered in this volume is that the story of Billingham's development is all too often unrecognised. It is a story of considerable vision and more than this it is a story of the pioneer spirit. Today I.C.I. is an international company of world renown yet it is all too easy to forget its comparatively small beginning, part of which is the story of the chemical industry at Billingham. The photographs in this book are a testimony to the tremendous work done by the early employees at that first factory, the 'Synthetic'. It is all too easy for historians to attribute praise for vision to those in the past, yet there is no doubt that these early pioneers at Billingham, forgotten names like George Pollitt, Roland Slade, Amos Cowap, Herbert Humphrey and Philip Dickens, with their never say die attitude, set out to transform those bare fields of long ago into the multi-operational chemical industry of today. As I write this, it is possible that the wheel has turned full circle and that there is a contracting chemical industry at Billingham, but this should not diminish the feats of the past. The discovery of anhydrite under Billingham was once described as a 'gift from the Gods'.[1] Divine gift it may well be, but I.C.I. is surely the miracle.

Of course the story of Billingham in the years between the wars is not just about I.C.I. Although the company became the dominant factor in the lives of many, the development of the town itself is surely another major example of enterprise and careful thought. The careful utilisation by Billingham Urban District Council of the economic miracle within the area to provide a town for 'living in' is a positive exaltation of the way in which industry and local government can work together for the benefit of all.

A BRIEF HISTORICAL NOTE

In 1915 with the vital supplies of nitrates from Chile threatened by the war H.M. Government decided to produce nitrates synthetically, using the recently discovered method of producing them from nitrogen in the air. The Ministry of Munitions obtained a site south east of Billingham. However the factory was never built and in 1919 the site was sold to Brunner Mond. The advent of industry led to Billingham Parish Council deciding to break away from Stockton Rural District Council. After much public debate Billingham Urban District was formed in 1923.

DEDICATION

I would like to dedicate this book to my grandfather Bill Menzies, my father Bob Menzies and my father-in-law E.F. (Frank) Bowen, who with 48, 35 and 39 years service respectively, all have a part in the history of I.C.I. and thus in that of Billingham. Also my wife Andrea and daughter Lara.

Billingham Parish Council.

BILLINGHAM VILLAGE
Peace Celebrations
SATURDAY, JULY 19th, 1919.

Programme.

9-15 a.m., Farmers' and Tradesmen's
Turn-outs and Cyclists
Assemble at North end of Wynyard Terrace.

9-30, Procession of above round the Village, by way
of South View, to The Green for Judging.

10-0, Assemble at St. Cuthbert's Cross.

SINGING OF NATIONAL ANTHEM.

God save our gracious King,
Long live our noble King,
God save the King.
Send him victorious,
Happy and glorious,
Long to reign over us,
God save the King.

God bless our native land!
May heaven's protecting hand
Still guard our shore:
May peace her power extend,
Foe be transformed to friend,
And Britain's power depend
On War no more.

PRESENTATION OF MEDALS TO SCHOOL CHILDREN.

10-15, Commence Children's Sports on the
Village Green, continuing until Mid-day.

1-30, First Event of Adult Sports and
continuation of Children's Sports.

3-45, Tea to all Children between the
ages of 3 and 14 years.

5-30, Continuation of Sports.

7-0, Singing Competitions.

7-30, Presentation of Prizes.

8-0, Dancing.

10-15, Fireworks.

A BAND WILL BE IN ATTENDANCE.

The Inhabitants are requested to make display of Flags
and Bunting.

God Save the King.

1. PEACE CELEBRATIONS 19 July 1919:

The idea of a Celebration was first mentioned by J. Bolton at a meeting of the Parish Council on 6 May 1919.[2] A special committee was set up on June 2 to organise the event and a full day of celebrations were organised as is shown in this programme. The Procession included children with their Sunday School teachers, all Friendly and other societies, Special Constables and 'Comrades of the Great War'. Tea consisting of two sandwiches, one jam tart, one piece of fruit cake and two small cakes was given to over 500 children. Prizes totalling £21.75 were won in the Sports and 1600 medals costing £23.86, were presented. In the evening, there was dancing on the Sports Field to the music of the band of Mr. R. Simmonds and the day ended with a firework display provided by Brocks.

2. MUNITIONS SITE 1919

The site acquired by Brunner Mond was described by Amos Cowap the Construction Manager as a 'good imitation of a Prairie'. There was plenty of roughshooting for invited guests including the Chairman of at least one local council! The only permanent buildings were the Tibbersley and Grange farmhouses together with two stores buildings erected by the Ministry. There were also some wooden huts and dumps of material together with three roads made by German prisoners of war[3]. This photo shows an ash path, which ran north from Grange farm passing close to some gas holder foundations built by the Ministry.

3. CONSTRUCTION OF THE SYNTHETIC FACTORY

An Executive Committee was set up in November 1920 with George Pollitt as Chief Executive. Pollitt soon became a major force in the Billingham project urging that 'housing, laboratory, new road, railway access . . . be hurried forward'.[4] By early 1921 contracts for housing in Mill Lane and the Roscoe Road/Crescent Avenue area were issued and work on the plant had also started. However in May 1921 Brunner announced a cut in their financial support because of industrial unrest and a trade depression. The Billingham project, shown here in construction, was kept alive only on a minimum budget by Pollitt but there had to be major changes. These included the Committee having to be content with plans for a temporary 'Scratch Plant'.

4. EARLY VIEW OF FACTORY TOWARDS HAVERTON ROAD c. 1925

The 'Scratch Plant' was renamed No. 2 Unit, but further labour problems prevented it becoming operational on schedule in January 1923. Undeterred, Pollitt pressed on with the construction plans and finally on Christmas Eve 1923 Dr. Roland Slade announced to the Executive that 'the first traces of ammonia had appeared at 11.30 p.m. on December 22nd[5]. By January 1924, the sulphate plant was operational and by 1925 'systematic development of the site with plants "capable of indefinite expansion"[6] was being planned. Within five years the factory was being acclaimed as 'one of the world's biggest' with an output of 2000 tons of nitrate per day.[7] This early view of the factory looks north with the road from Billingham to Haverton Hill and the L.N.E.R. railway to Port Clarence beyond the factory. Middle Belasis farm is also shown.

5. CHILTON'S LANE 1926

Several projects ancillary to the design and erection of plants were ongoing in the mid 1920's. A major plan was for the construction of the Main Office in Chilton's Lane. Work began in early 1926 and the construction (shown here) was by Lumsdens of Newcastle. By May 1927 the offices were fully occupied. Chilton's Lane was officially closed to the public on 30 March 1925 when New Road was finally completed. Shortly after this Chilton's Lane was straightened, having been a winding lane passing through the site, a step which for many 'marked the decisive step from a country site to an industrial area'[8]. This view looks towards the village with Chilton's Lane in the foreground and the new housing south of the lane is also visible. Several landmarks can be seen in the village including the Brewery Chimney, the church tower, and in the distance, Billingham Hall.

6. VIEW FROM THE CHURCH TOWER c. 1926

This definitive view provides a good impression of the physical geography of the farmland east and south east of Billingham before it was developed. The new factory, the 'Synthetic', the Main Office and new housing between Chilton's Lane and Mill Lane are all shown, as is Belasis Lane, here merely a country lane to Haverton Hill. Plans for 1000 houses north of Belasis Lane were formed in 1927[9] with the first part of the scheme for 485 houses and a road to run through the estate from Station Road to Belasis Lane and Cowpen Lane (this was Central Avenue) being approved in 1928[10].

7. VIEW FROM THE CHURCH TOWER c. 1935

By 1930 600 properties were being erected north east of Billingham Station[11], houses were being erected north of Belasis Lane and more expansion was being planned with the planned acquisition of land 'between the two railways' for what was to become Cowpen Estate.[12] This view almost a decade later shows clearly the development around the old village. Great tracts of agricultural land were swallowed up by housing developments and the North Eastern Evening Gazette told of 'Billingham's Amazing Growth' reporting that the 'mushroom town trebles population in four years'.[13]

8. I.C.I. OFFICES c. 1928

Late in 1926 it became known that the four largest chemical companies in Britain were to merge and on 7th December 1926 the name Imperial Chemical Industries Ltd. was registered. Pollitt was elected to the new Board and ceased to have full time responsibility at Billingham. In October 1927 Synthetic was reorganised as a subsidiary company with a Management Executive of seven men, led by Dr. Roland Slade. This photograph of the Main Office is interesting in that it is one of the earliest ones taken after the merger and this is reflected in the title on the picture.

9. SYNTHETIC OFFICES c. 1926

This is the Main Office as it nears completion with the temporary huts used by employees also visible. For many years 'the great Tees-side factory was popularly known' as the 'Synthetic'[14] and this is reflected here in the title given to this picture.

10. BILLINGHAM GREEN TOWARDS THE PINNACLE c. 1929

This is a view of the row of cottages that stood on the south side of the Green opposite the Church of England school. At the end of South Row the Lych Gate can be seen together with one of Billingham's more unusual buildings, Tower House or the 'Pinnacle' as it was known locally. Built of white brick it was 60 feet high and thought to have been erected c. 1870 by George Robson. He had originally wished to build in a horizontal direction along the Green, but this was objected to by the local authorities. Robson is reputed to have said that if they wouldn't let him build along then he would build up![15]. The building was described as dilapidated in 1939[16] and despite calls then for its demolition it survived until the 1960's.

11. NORTH ROW AND SCHOOL HOUSE c. 1929

This shows the cottages on the north side of the Green with the School House standing at the end of North Row. Next to the School House stands a 'Thompson style' farmhouse, one of several village farms dating from the late eighteenth century. In fact this is the only building from the east side of the Green that still stands in 1986. The house on the end of North Row was demolished in 1932 to make way for the new Methodist Chapel.

12. POOL'S GARAGE c. 1930's

This garage was an eighteenth century building[17] adjoining Tower House opposite Fletcher's shop. The picture also provides a fine view of the eighteenth century cottages that stood in Church Row. Described as having 'huge low-built rafters ... carved from oak ... taken from old wind-jammers',[18] one of these cottages had been used as the village Post Office in the early years of this century[19]. Some of these were later demolished in 1939 and replaced by the church hall, whilst the other cottages still stand today, although they are now in a dilapidated state.

13. BILLINGHAM GREEN c. 1927

This busy scene is viewed from a point outside the Smiths Arms and looks south east towards the village school and Town End Farm. To the left of the farm, is the row of houses on the east side of the Green including Brewery House, the Georgian building that stood in front of the Brewery chimney. Brewery House contained in 1927, a kitchen, two large sitting rooms as well as four very large bedrooms.[20] On the right of the picture Fletcher's van can just be seen waiting at the side of the shop. Unfortunately the horse and cart in the foreground are only a blurred image.

14. THE SMITHS ARMS, BILLINGHAM c. 1928

This photograph looks north across the Green towards Chapel Road and Station Road. It shows the Smiths Arms prior to the present building. Plans from Messrs. J.W. Cameron and Co. Ltd. to build the present building were approved in March 1929.[21] Also shown at the end of North Row, is Cooper's Grocery Shop with a delivery van waiting outside. Along with the rest of North Row, it was demolished in the early 1960's.

15. THE SCHOOL, BILLINGHAM GREEN c. 1929

This view is looking east from outside the church towards the Church of England School on the Green with the village cross in the foreground. Both the school and cross were erected in the nineteenth century.[22] By 1926 the rapid post war increase in children had led to demands for more schools. Plans were passed in 1927 for another school on a site in Belasis Lane[23] and this became Billingham Intermediate School when it opened in the early 1930's. A new Church of England Infants School was also opened in June 1929.

16. THE PARK, BILLINGHAM c. 1929

This photograph looks northwards towards South View and Belasis Lane with the end of Town End Farm also visible and a Blumer's bus also shown. There had been a duck pond at the junction of Belasis and Mill Lane as far back as 1775,[24] but by the late 1920's it had become a 'stinking mess in need of great attention'.[25] The Council in an attempt to rectify this situation created a Park with a shrubbery and a paddling pool.[26] In May 1930, a new Co-operative Stores building was opened on the site of Town End Farm. The thirtieth shop of the Stockton Society with a shop frontage of 270 feet it was perhaps a forerunner of the present shopping centre idea as it had eight different shops ranging from a butcher to a barber and a Public Hall seating 650 people.[27]

17. THE PICTURE HOUSE, BILLINGHAM c. 1932

Plans for a cinema to be built on the corner of Mill Lane and South View, were approved in February 1928.[28] Here the 'Billingham Picture House' costing £10,000 and accommodating approximately 700 people, was opened on 8 October 1928. The Managing Director was a Mr. R.S. Groves of Eaglescliffe and the programme for the Grand opening night was the 'popular comedy "The Kid Brother" with Harold Lloyd followed by a performance of the Synthetic Male Voice Choir'.[29]

18. MILL LANE c. 1928

The first new housing developments were close to the factory in Mill Lane, Roscoe Road and Crescent Avenue, being built between 1922 and 1925. These were added to by 1927 with Imperial Road, Mond Crescent, Brunner Road and New Road being constructed.[30] The Council minutes for 1927-1928 reflect this growth around Mill Lane with a large number of plans for commercial development being approved. In 1928 a 'fine new shopping centre (was) . . . being built to cope with the demands of an ever growing population'.[31] and by December 1928 it was reported that 'between 20 to 30 brightly decorated shop windows stood where . . . there was not a single establishment six months ago'.[32]

19. THE GARDEN CITY c. 1928

This photograph shows West Avenue, part of the Garden City, the 73 houses built by the Newcastle upon Tyne Electric Supply Company in 1917. Although this provision of housing for the influx of labour was continued by the Synthetic, there was concern over the housing situation.[33] By 1929 over 14,000 were employed at the new factory and the drive for more houses was beginning to take up land north of the old village[34] as well as beyond Billingham Station[35].

20. THE GARDEN CITY c. 1928

This photograph and the one on the previous page are part of the Garden Village, the most modern housing at the time it was erected. The estate had electric lighting and facilities for cooking using electricity. The whole area was planned with the aim of being artistically pleasing, every house having a garden. There was continued integration between the new industry and the council with men such as A.T.S. Zealley, Works Manager in the Synthetic, becoming prominent figures in the work of the local council.[36]

21. WIDENING BILLINGHAM BANK 1 OCTOBER 1929

With Billingham's increasing importance both as an industrial centre and as a town, it soon became clear that some of its roads were quite inadequate. One was the road from Norton to Billingham originally the turnpike road to Sunderland built to replace Old Road in the late eighteenth century. In October 1928 the Council pressed for the scheme to widen the road from Norton to Billingham, to be commenced with some urgency[37] and this photograph shows Billingham Bank being widened with the difference between the width of the old road and the new road being clearly shown.

22. BILLINGHAM BANK c. 1929.

This view of the Norton to Billingham Road shows Billingham Bank in the distance. Also shown is the new housing development along Hill Road and Bank Road, off Billingham Bank. These were 'staff houses' for employees of the 'Synthetic' and four houses were completed in Hill Road by mid-1926, whilst a further seven staff houses were built on Bank Road in 1927 by Lumsdens of Newcastle, the contractor for the Main Office.

23. HIGH GRANGE FARM (front) c. 1928

Although there was an emphasis on industrial development at this time there was still a number of working farms in Billingham, particularly north of the station. One was High Grange Farm which stood on the site of what is now the Stockton and Billingham Technical College. The farm consisted of almost 500 acres and had been farmed by Frederick Bell since 1900.

24. HIGH GRANGE FARM AND THE MOOR c. 1928

The farm is seen here from the rear across the rough area to the east of the farm known as 'the moor'. Until the land between the farm and the railway line was used for housing in the late 1920's and early 1930's it had been possible to sit in the farmhouse and see Billingham church. During the Great War the bombing of the Hartlepools was visible from the farm. Within the farmhouse itself there was no electricity or gas so candles and oil lamps were used for light, with coal fires being used for cooking and heat.

25. FARMER BELL c. 1929

Frederick Bell was a keen horseman regularly joining the hunt at Wolviston to 'draw Noddings whin and the Fox Covert east of Bell's farm'. An occasion is recalled by Alan Bell when a fox ran from Bell's farm across the Wolviston Road and Northfield Farm eventually escaping in Wynyard wood. As well as being Church Warden for 23 years, Frederick Bell had also been a Special Constable during the Great War although the Army had forced him to sell his favourite mount 'Little Chilton' for £70 in 1915.

26. FARMER BELL PLOUGHING IN FRONT OF WOLVISTON GRANGE c. 1930

This is an interesting photograph because it shows the area around the Swan Hotel prior to any sort of development. In the distance can be seen Wolviston Grange Farm which stood where Sidlaw Road and Grosmont Road are today. The road to Wolviston then only a country road, is also visible. As well as arable farming the Bell's supplied milk to the workhouse in Portrack, children's homes in Stockton and delivered to private customers in the large houses such as Greenholme that stood on the Wolviston Road. They regularly took their farm produce across the Transporter for sale at shops including Walter Wilson's in Middlesbrough.

27. BILLINGHAM HALL c. 1931

This is a view of the Hall taken by Leslie Dixon of the Dixon family, residents of Glebe Farm in the village. They farmed the fields adjacent to the Hall and beyond the station up on the west of Wolviston Road. The Hall was erected in the early 1870's[38] and here, it is in its final years as it was to be demolished in 1935 to make way for the building of Conifer Crescent.

28. LUNCH IN THE FIELDS: 'THE DIXONS', c. 1928

North of Billingham there had been little development before 1930. Around the Station and west of the Wolviston Road along Sandy Lane, there was only farmland and here the Dixons farmed. The family gained considerable fame in the agricultural world through their exploits in ploughing. Tom Dixon came to Glebe Farm, Billingham in May 1904 and won 262 ploughing championships. Here Tom, with sons leslie and John and some of their farm labourers, have lunch, taken in the fields because it was too far to walk back to the farmhouse in the village. Behind the group is Billingham Station.

29. GETTING IN THE HARVEST c. 1929

This is the Dixon family again and they are hard at work gathering the harvest in the field between Billingham Hall and Billingham Station. Leslie Dixon followed in the footsteps of his father, gaining frame in Britain and abroad for his exploits in ploughing. He even travelled to Canada to take part in ploughing championships. The Dixons were well known in the village and their eventual move away from farming, like that of others like the Bell family, as they gradually lost their farmland to the ever encroaching urban development, was really a testimony to the diminishing role of agriculture in the area.

30. 'A BRIEF REST' c. 1929

This photograph again shows a group of workers on the Dixon farm having a break from their work. The signal box at Billingham Station and Billingham Hall can be seen clearly behind the group. This area is now all part of the Conifer Crescent development.

31. SANDY LANE c. 1929

Until just after the Great War, Sandy Lane was in fact a gated road with one gate near the junction with Wolviston Road and one past the junction with the lane going up to Northfield Farm. The first houses on Sandy Lane were built in the late 1920's near the junction with the Wolviston Road and until the mid 1930's marked the northern limit of the development of Billingham. Here Leslie Dixon is on the tractor and in the distance the new houses are being erected at the top of Sandy Lane.

32. WOLVISTON ROAD c. 1930

Wolviston Road was a country lane with little development, apart from three houses called Greenholme, Ashtree Cottage and Winford House, until the expansion of the housing programme north of Billingham Station in the late 1920's. There were a small group of houses erected close to the junction of Sandy Lane and the Wolviston Road in 1929, and these can be seen behind this group of workers. The major development was that of High Grange Estate (Roseberry Estate) in 1935. The houses, built by Harland and Parker, were sold for between £395 and £580[39]. Roseberry Road was part of this development extending east from Wolviston Road although it terminated at the fields of High Grange Farm, still a working farm at this time.

33. DIXON'S MILK ROUND c. 1929

The Dixon's took their milk out each day around the village and up to Billingham Hall where they left seven pints on occasion. They used a horse to draw the milk cart up until the 1930's. Here is one of their carts outside the farm.

34. LESLIE DIXON WITH LORRY c. 1934

Leslie was a natural mechanic and he related many tales to me about some of his early exploits. Here he is with one of the Dixons lorries, a familiar sight in Billingham between the wars. Billingham Social Club is in the background.

35. WORKMEN CONSTRUCTING COWPEN LANE c. 1930

The old Cowpen Lane went from the junction with Belasis Lane, east of the present road crossing the railway to Port Clarence past the site of the old Clarence Brick Works (this became Charlton's Pond) and continued to Cowpen Bewley. Plans were submitted in May 1930 for a diversion of the old Cowpen Lane from Belasis Lane, crossing the L.N.E.R. line by a new bridge 45 feet wide with a span of 69 feet and rejoining the existing road north of the bridge at a point known as the 'straight mile'.[40]

36. COWPEN LANE c. 1930

As well as plans for the diversion of old Cowpen Lane plans were also submitted for the widening of the old road.[41] This was in conjunction with a major development of the Cowpen Lane area with the Council having purchased 46.631 acres of land from the Ecclesiastical commissioners at a cost of £12,235 for the purpose of erecting 566 houses.[42] The development was in several parts with the first houses, built by Messrs. Stephen Coates Ltd. of Middlesbrough,[43] being occupied in January 1931.

37. OLD COWPEN LANE CROSSING c. 1928

The line from Billingham to Port Clarence built in 1833[44] crossed old Cowpen Lane at a point which today is the end of Hereford Terrace. This lane was once the route from Greatham to Billingham passing through Cowpen Bewley village. South of the crossing was the new 'Synthetic' factory and it is just visible in the background of this photograph.

38. COWPEN LANE AND BILLINGHAM SCHOOL c. 1931

This photograph of old Cowpen Lane was taken at a point just north of the junction of Belasis Lane and shows clearly the poor condition of the road at that time. In the distance is Billingham Intermediate School, at that time only recently constructed.

39. TOP OF CENTRAL AVENUE c. 1931

Land for the construction of a road to run from Station Road to Belasis Avenue through the new housing development north of Belasis Lane had first been surveyed with a view to acquisition in June 1927.[45] The road was within the initial part of this development in 1928-1929 and was named Central Avenue. With two carriageways, each 20 feet wide and a 9 foot wide central verge with trees, it was praised as an 'excellent example of modern town planning'.[46]

40. THE DEMOLITION OF THE BREWERY CHIMNEY 4 DECEMBER 1937

The Brewery Chimney had been one of the landmarks in the village since the nineteenth century as the Heslop brewery business was noted as far back as 1858.[47] The demolition of the chimney marked the end of Billingham's own brewery.

THE PHOTOGRAPHER considered himself fortunate when he arrived too late for the felling of the 70ft. chimney of Billingham Old Brewery, which is being demolished for a site for a new cinema. The stack fell unexpectedly and out of its estimated position, damaging these stables of Billingham Co-operative Society—from the roof of which the only possible view of the felling of the himney could have been taken.

41. DEVELOPMENT ON THE SITE OF BILLINGHAM HALL 12 FEBRUARY 1935

After Billingham Hall was demolished building began immediately of a new housing estate by Kendrews (Builders) Ltd., of Middlesbrough. Today this is the Conifer Crescent development and this photograph shows the building in progress. This was further evidence of the expansion of Billingham north of the original village settlement.

42. SKATING ON ICE ON BILLINGHAM BOTTOMS c. 1935

Many people who lived in Billingham in the years before the Second World War have memories of skating on the land between Billingham and Norton, popularly known as Billingham Bottoms. As can be seen from the photograph it was certainly a popular pastime and people actually came from many other villages to take part in the fun.

43. STATION ROAD c. 1934

Station Road was a country lane prior to the Great War with Billingham Hall to the west along with allotments between the Hall and the village. The land east of the road was mainly farmland until it was developed in the late 1920's and this photograph shows the houses immediately south of Billingham Station.

44. TRAFFIC CHAOS AT BILLINGHAM STATION 19 NOVEMBER 1938

With the development of the 'Synthetic' and the subsequent daily influx of labour into the Billingham area, there was regular traffic chaos in Station Road at the level crossing, due to the frequency of railway traffic passing through Billingham. As early as 1931, a possible by-pass was being proposed to help with the difficulties faced by traffic at Billingham Station.[48] The debate was still continuing in 1935 when it was reported that, considerable agitation for a by-pass road had 'been in evidence for some time'.[49]

45. SANDY LANE AT HARVEST TIME c. 1938

This is again the Dixon family engaged in the work of harvesting close to Sandy Lane. It is perhaps a fitting reminder, as this book in terms of its own chronology, approaches the Second World War, of Billingham's close links with agriculture. After 1945 there was further expansion of the town and Billingham entered a third stage of development with a revolutionary Town Centre and a huge housing programme east of the A19 road, a final confirmation of the creation of a new town away from the old village settlement.

46. H.R.H. THE PRINCE OF WALES VISITS BILLINGHAM JULy 1930

The Prince of Wales, later Edward VIII, visited Billingham on 2 July 1930 coming mainly to see the new industrial development in the town. The Prince having already been to the Brittania Works at Dorman Long, crossed the Tees to Billingham alighting at Bamlett's Wharf. After being met by Lord Londonderry the Lord Lieutenant of County Durham, Lord Melchett the Chairman of I.C.I. and the Chief Constable of Durham, the Prince met the directors of Synthetic Ammonia and Nitrates Ltd. before touring the factory.

47. H.R.H. THE PRINCE OF WALES AT BILLINGHAM

The Prince went on to visit the recently built I.C.I. Sports Pavillion walking across the new Sports Field expressing his delight at these new ventures. He then passed on to the Main Offices where he met members of Billingham Urban District Council and the Office staff who were lined up outside. Thousands of I.C.I. employees cheered him on as he passed to his next appointment at Stockton, half an hour late.[50] This royal seal of approval must have been welcomed by both I.C.I. and the members of the Urban District Council, a culmination of the development of both industry and local administration within the new town.

48. THE VISIT OF H.R.H. KING GEORGE VI AND H.R.H. QUEEN ELIZABETH 19 JUNE 1941

A less publicised royal visit took place during the Second World War when the King and Queen came to Billingham and visited I.C.I. They were here to see the vital production carried out by the factory and this was in fact one of their few wartime visits to Teesside.

49. FLETCHER'S BACON ADVERT FROM THE 1930's

This is one of eighteen different advertisements for Fletcher's grocery shop that used to be shown in the interval in the programme of films at the Billingham Picture House between the years 1931 and 1940. They were drawn originally by Henry Eldon Fletcher and he sent them to Leeds to be made up into slides.